salads

© ACP Magazines Ltd 2006

This 2010 edition published by Fall River Press,
by arrangement with ACP Books, a division of ACP Magazines Ltd,
a division of PBL Media Limited.

Cover Lobster and soba salad with ponzu dressing, page 98
Back cover Ocean trout and asparagus salad with creamy horseradish
dressing, page 96
Photographer Chris Chen
Stylist Kirsty Cassidy
Home economist Sammie Coryton

Fall River Press
122 Fifth Avenue
New York, NY 10011

ISBN: 978-1-4351-2469-1

Printed and bound in China

10 9 8 7 6 5 4 3 2 1

salads

Pamela Clark

FALL RIVER PRESS

contents

introduction

To produce a cookbook dedicated to fresh and delicious salads is a delight. But, these are not just side salads— they are complete meals. Chicken, beef, or seafood; pasta, rice, or noodles; combinations of fruit and vegetables—the ingredients are substantial and varied. And the flavors we've embraced from all over the world have given the salad a new lease of life.

Pamela Clark

vegetarian

Some people just think of a salad in terms of a bowl of green leaves. In this section we show how versatile, colorful, and tempting a vegetarian salad can be.

a new leaf...

mesclun is a salad mixture of assorted
young lettuces and other green leaves

Romaine lettuce is the traditional Caesar salad lettuce

Boston lettuce has soft, papery leaves

baby Romaine lettuce is a miniature version of Romaine lettuce, and has slightly bitter leaves

red and green leaf lettuces have tightly curled, crunchy leaves, each with a distinct taste

iceberg lettuce a heavy, firm lettuce with tightly packed leaves and a crisp texture

red Boston lettuce has crisp, tightly furled leaves and a slightly bitter taste

green leaf and red oak lettuces have a delicate flavor

radicchio a member of the chicory family used in Italian cooking as well as salads

arugula has a spicy, slightly peppery flavor

baby arugula more delicate both in flavor and in texture than ordinary rocket

wild rocket deep-green serrated leaves, with a stronger flavor and scent than rocket

curly endive also known as frisée, has a loose head of frilly, slightly bitter leaves

lamb's lettuce also known as mâche or corn salad, has tender, nutty-tasting leaves

spinach has a more delicate texture and taste than Swiss chard

Chinese cabbage also known as Peking cabbage, has elongated, crinkly leaves

watercress a member of the mustard family, has a peppery, bitter flavor

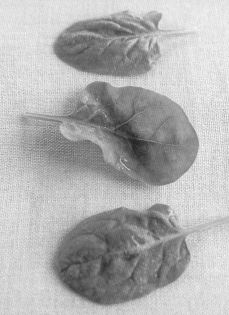

baby spinach softer than spinach, used raw in salads or cooked in risottos

fennel tastes like licorice and is great raw or cooked

Belgian endive can be white or red; has a bittersweet flavor

baby bok choy is distinctively acrid but has very tender leaves

beet, squash and spinach salad with feta polenta

2 cups water
2 cups vegetable stock
1 cup polenta
7 ounces feta cheese, crumbled
10 small beets (about 1¼ pounds)
3 tablespoons olive oil
1½ pounds peeled butternut
squash, diced into 1½-inch
pieces
5 cups baby spinach
¾ cup toasted walnuts, chopped
coarsely

WALNUT VINAIGRETTE
3 tablespoons walnut oil
¼ cup olive oil
¼ cup lemon juice

1 Preheat oven to 400. Grease 8- x 12-inch baking pan; line with parchment paper.

2 Combine the water and stock in large pot; bring to a boil. Gradually add polenta, stirring constantly. Reduce heat; cook, stirring, about 10 minutes or until polenta thickens. Stir in cheese then spread polenta into prepared pan. Cool 10 minutes then cover; refrigerate about 1 hour or until polenta is firm.

3 Meanwhile, discard beet stems and leaves; quarter unpeeled beets then place in large shallow baking dish; drizzle with half of the oil. Roast, uncovered, about 15 minutes. Add squash; drizzle with remaining oil. Roast, uncovered, about 30 minutes or until vegetables are tender.

4 Whisk together ingredients for walnut vinaigrette.

5 When cool enough to handle, peel beets. Place in large bowl with dressing; toss gently to combine.

6 Turn polenta onto cutting board; trim edges. Cut polenta into 12 pieces; cook, in batches, on heated oiled grill or grill pan until browned on both sides and heated through.

7 Add squash, spinach, and nuts to beet mixture; toss gently to combine. Divide polenta pieces among serving plates; top with salad.

preparation time 20 minutes
(plus refrigeration time)
cooking time 1 hour 15 minutes
serves 4

per serving 59.8g fat; 839 cal

hot rigatoni salad with cauliflower

Rigatoni—ridged, hollow tubes of pasta that look like a short, fat version of penne—are a perfect shape to capture and hold the sauce in this recipe.

12 ounces rigatoni
⅓ cup extra virgin olive oil
5 cloves garlic, chopped coarsely
1½ cups stale breadcrumbs
12 ounces cauliflower florets
12 ounces broccoli florets
⅓ cup lemon juice
1 cup coarsely chopped fresh, flat-leaf parsley
½ cup toasted sliced almonds

1 Cook pasta in large pot of boiling water, uncovered, until just tender.

2 Meanwhile, heat 3 tablespoons of the oil in large skillet; cook garlic and breadcrumbs, stirring, until browned lightly. Place in large serving bowl.

3 Heat remaining oil in same skillet; cook cauliflower and broccoli, in batches, stirring, until almost tender. Add vegetables to bowl with drained pasta, lemon juice, parsley, and nuts; toss to combine.

preparation time 25 minutes
cooking time 15 minutes
serves 4

per serving 26.3g fat; 683 cal

sesame omelet and crisp mixed vegetable salad

8 eggs
½ cup milk
½ cup coarsely chopped fresh
  garlic chives
3 tablespoons toasted sesame
  seeds
8 cups (about 1¼ pounds) finely
  shredded Chinese cabbage
2 fresh long red chilies, seeded,
  sliced thinly
1 large red bell pepper, sliced
  thinly
1 large green bell pepper, sliced
  thinly
1½ tablespoons coarsely
  chopped fresh mint
1½ tablespoons finely chopped
fresh lemongrass

SWEET CHILI DRESSING
2 teaspoons toasted sesame
  seeds
¼ cup rice vinegar
¼ cup peanut oil
1 teaspoon sesame oil
¼ cup sweet Thai chili sauce

1 Whisk eggs in large measuring cup with milk, chives, and seeds until well combined. Pour a quarter of the egg mixture into heated lightly oiled wok or large skillet; cook over medium heat, tilting skillet, until omelet is just set. Remove from wok; repeat with remaining egg mixture to make four omelets. Roll cooled omelets tightly; cut into ¼-inch "wheels."
2 Whisk together ingredients for sweet chili dressing.
3 Place three-quarters of the omelet in large bowl with cabbage, chilies, bell peppers, mint, lemongrass, and dressing; toss gently to combine. Divide salad among serving plates; top with remaining omelets.

preparation time 25 minutes
cooking time 10 minutes
serves 4

per serving 31.1g fat; 396 cal

tip
Omelets can be made up to 3 hours ahead and stored, covered, in the refrigerator. Roll and slice just before assembling the salad.

grilled haloumi, asparagus and arugula salad

Haloumi is a firm cheese that can be cooked for brief periods of time without breaking down.

5 ounces baby green beans, trimmed
1½ tablespoons olive oil
1 pound asparagus, halved crosswise
1 pound haloumi cheese, sliced thinly
1 large avocado, sliced thinly
½ cup toasted macadamia nuts, chopped coarsely
7 cups arugula

MACADAMIA DRESSING
1 teaspoon mild English mustard
¼ cup macadamia oil
¼ cup sherry vinegar

1 Whisk together ingredients for macadamia dressing.

2 Boil, steam, or microwave beans until just tender; drain. Rinse under cold water; drain.

3 Meanwhile, heat half of the oil in large skillet; cook asparagus, in batches, until just tender.

4 Heat remaining oil in same skillet; cook cheese, in batches, until browned on both sides. Drain on paper towels.

5 Place beans, asparagus, and cheese in large bowl with avocado, nuts, arugula, and dressing; toss gently to combine.

preparation time 20 minutes
cooking time 15 minutes
serves 4

per serving 67.4g fat; 765 cal

tip
Haloumi must be browned just before serving or it becomes leathery and unpalatable.

sesame tofu salad

Kalonji, also known as nigella, are angular seeds, black on the outside and creamy within, having a sharp nutty flavor. They can be found in specialty spice shops and Middle Eastern food stores.

two 10½-ounce blocks firm silken tofu
3 tablespoons toasted sesame seeds
3 tablespoons kalonji
2 teaspoons dried chili flakes
3 tablespoons cornstarch
vegetable oil, for deep-frying
5 green onions, sliced thinly
1 large avocado, chopped coarsely
3½ cups red leaf lettuce, torn
3½ cups mizuna, arugula, or young mustard greens
1 fresh long red chili, seeded, sliced thinly

SESAME DRESSING
2 shallots, chopped finely
3 tablespoons toasted sesame seeds
1½ tablespoons sesame oil
1½ tablespoons kecap manis
½-inch piece fresh ginger, grated
¼ cup lemon juice

1 Whisk together ingredients for sesame dressing.
2 Cut each tofu block lengthwise into four slices; dry gently with paper towels. Combine sesame and kalonji seeds, chili, and cornstarch in large shallow bowl; press seed mixture onto both sides of tofu slices.
3 Heat oil in wok or large pot; deep-fry tofu, in batches, until browned lightly. Drain on paper towels.
4 Place remaining ingredients in large bowl; toss gently to combine. Divide salad among serving plates; top with tofu, drizzle with dressing.

preparation time 25 minutes
cooking time 10 minutes
serves 4

per serving 45.9g fat; 542 cal

tip
You can find kecap manis at Asian markets, or you can make your own by heating equal parts soy sauce and brown sugar or molasses, stirring until the sugar or molasses dissolves.

fattoush

6 pocket pitas
olive oil, for shallow-frying
3 medium tomatoes (about
  1 pound), chopped coarsely
1 large green bell pepper,
chopped coarsely
2 small cucumbers, seeded,
  sliced thinly
10 trimmed red radishes, sliced
  thinly
4 spring onions, sliced thinly
1½ cups firmly packed fresh
  flat-leaf parsley
½ cup coarsely chopped fresh
  mint

LEMON GARLIC DRESSING
2 cloves garlic, crushed
¼ cup olive oil
¼ cup lemon juice

1 Whisk together ingredients for lemon garlic dressing.

2 Halve pita horizontally; cut into 1-inch pieces. Heat oil in wok or large skillet; shallow-fry pita in batches until browned lightly and crisp. Drain on paper towels.

3 Just before serving, place about three-quarters of the pita in large bowl with dressing and remaining ingredients; toss gently to combine. Sprinkle remaining pita over fattoush.

preparation time 30 minutes
cooking time 5 minutes
serves 4

per serving 30.6g fat; 630 cal

tips
Chop mint just before serving to prevent it from discoloring.

For a lower-fat alternative, spray pita pieces with cooking-oil spray then bake, uncovered, in hot oven until crisp; break into small pieces over salad.

tortellini and ribbon-vegetable salad with lemon dijon dressing

4 large carrots
3 medium zucchini
2 medium fennel bulbs (about
    1¼ pounds)
1 medium red onion
12 ounces spinach and ricotta
    tortellini
3 tablespoons coarsely chopped
    fennel-frond tips
7 ounces feta cheese, crumbled

LEMON DIJON DRESSING
2 teaspoons Dijon mustard
2 teaspoons sugar
½ cup lemon juice
¼ cup olive oil

1 Using sharp knife, v-slicer, or mandoline, slice vegetables thinly; place in large heatproof bowl. Cover with boiling water; let stand 30 seconds, drain. Rinse under cold water; drain.

2 Cook pasta in large pot of boiling water, uncovered, until just tender; drain.

3 Meanwhile, whisk together ingredients for lemon Dijon dressing.

4 Place vegetables and pasta in large bowl with fennel tips, cheese, and dressing; toss gently to combine.

preparation time 25 minutes
cooking time 10 minutes
serves 4

per serving 29.6g fat; 500 cal

grilled herb polenta with sun-dried tomato and olive salad

2 cups water
2 cups prepared vegetable stock
1 cup polenta
⅓ cup finely grated parmesan
  cheese
1½ tablespoons finely chopped
  fresh flat-leaf parsley
1½ tablespoons finely chopped
  fresh basil

SUN-DRIED TOMATO AND OLIVE SALAD
3½ ounces baby romaine lettuce,
trimmed, leaves torn roughly
1⅓ cups drained sun-dried
  tomatoes
4 green onions, sliced thinly
¼ cup thinly sliced pitted black
  olives

SPICED MAYONNAISE
¾ cup mayonnaise
pinch cayenne pepper
¼ teaspoon ground cumin
¼ teaspoon ground coriander
¼ teaspoon ground turmeric
1½ tablespoons lemon juice

1 Combine the water and stock in medium pot; bring to a boil. Gradually add polenta to liquid, stirring constantly. Reduce heat; cook, stirring, about 10 minutes or until polenta thickens. Stir in cheese, parsley, and basil.

2 Spread polenta evenly into deep 8-inch-square cake pan; cool 10 minutes. Cover; refrigerate about 3 hours or until firm.

3 Turn polenta onto cutting board; trim edges. Cut into four squares, cut each square diagonally into two triangles. Cook polenta, in batches, on heated oiled grill or grill pan until browned on both sides.

4 Meanwhile, combine ingredients for sun-dried tomato and olive salad in medium bowl. Whisk together ingredients for spiced mayonnaise in small bowl until combined. Divide polenta among serving plates; top with salad, then drizzle with spiced mayonnaise mixture.

preparation time 15 minutes (plus refrigeration time)
cooking time 30 minutes
serves 4

per serving 25.7g fat; 539 cal

date and orange salad

1½ cups couscous
1½ cups boiling water
12 fresh dates, seeded, quartered
1 cup toasted walnuts, chopped
    coarsely
1½ tablespoons olive oil
1½ tablespoons walnut oil
2 large grapefruit (about
    2 pounds), peeled, sliced thinly
2 medium oranges (about
    1 pound), peeled, sliced thinly
14 trimmed red radishes, sliced
    thinly
3 cups mizuna, arugula, or young
    mustard greens
2 cups loosely packed fresh mint
2 cups loosely packed fresh
    cilantro

WALNUT OIL DRESSING
½ cup orange juice
2 teaspoons sugar
3 tablespoons walnut oil
3 tablespoons olive oil
½ teaspoon ground cinnamon

1 Combine couscous with the water in large heatproof bowl; cover, let stand about 5 minutes or until water is absorbed, fluffing with fork occasionally. Cool 10 minutes; stir in dates, nuts, and oils.

2 Whisk together ingredients for walnut oil dressing.

3 Add grapefruit, oranges, radishes, mizuna, and herbs to couscous mixture with dressing; toss gently to combine.

preparation time 40 minutes
serves 4

per serving 46.9g fat; 860 cal

brown rice, chickpea and pumpkin-seed salad with mixed-potato patties

1½ cups brown rice
1 large sweet potato (about 1 pound), chopped coarsely
4 small potatoes, chopped coarsely
3 tablespoons flour
3 tablespoons sour cream
3 tablespoons finely chopped fresh chives
¼ cup flour, extra
3 tablespoons vegetable oil
10½-ounce can chickpeas, rinsed, drained
⅓ cup pumpkin seeds
⅓ cup raisins
3 trimmed celery stalks, sliced thinly
3 tablespoons finely chopped fresh flat-leaf parsley
¼ cup finely chopped fresh mint
1½ tablespoons finely grated lemon peel
1 medium red onion, sliced thinly
3 small tomatoes, chopped finely

TAHINI DRESSING
3 tablespoons tahini
½ cup lemon juice
¼ cup olive oil

1 Cook rice in large pot of boiling water, uncovered, until rice is tender; drain. Rinse under cold water; drain.

2 Meanwhile, boil, steam, or microwave sweet potato and potatoes, separately, until tender; drain. Mash combined sweet potato and potatoes in large bowl; cool 10 minutes.

3 Whisk together ingredients for tahini dressing.

4 Stir flour, sour cream, and chives into mashed potato mixture. Shape mixture by hand into eight patties; coat patties in extra flour. Heat oil in large heavy-based skillet; cook patties, four at a time, until browned lightly on both sides and heated through. Cover to keep warm.

5 Place rice in large bowl with dressing and remaining ingredients; toss gently to combine. Serve rice salad with patties.

preparation time 20 minutes
cooking time 35 minutes
serves 4

per serving 43.3g fat; 967 cal

tip
Dried roasted pumpkin seeds are popular both as a cooking ingredient or eaten on their own as a snack.

poultry

Chicken, quail, duck, and turkey pieces make delicious, easy meals when combined with a salad of green leaves, grilled vegetables, pasta, and a delicious dressing.

smoked chicken and artichoke salad with caper dressing

2 medium yellow bell peppers
4 baby eggplants, sliced thinly
2 large zucchini, sliced thinly
3 tablespoons olive oil
12-ounce jar marinated quartered artichokes, drained
1 pound smoked chicken breasts, sliced thinly
14 ounces watercress, trimmed

CAPER DRESSING

2 hard-boiled eggs, quartered
1½ tablespoons drained capers
3 tablespoons white wine vinegar
3 tablespoons coarsely chopped fresh oregano
1 clove garlic, quartered
⅓ cup olive oil

1 Quarter bell peppers; discard seeds and membranes. Roast under broiler or at 475 degrees, skin-side up, until skin blisters and blackens. Cover bell pepper pieces with plastic wrap or aluminum foil for 5 minutes; peel away skin, then slice bell pepper thinly.

2 Meanwhile, make caper dressing.

3 Brush eggplants and zucchini with oil; cook, in batches, on heated oiled grill or grill pan until browned lightly and just tender; cool.

4 Place bell peppers, eggplants, and zucchini in large bowl with artichokes, chicken and dressing; toss gently to combine. Serve salad on watercress.

caper dressing Blend or process eggs, capers, vinegar, oregano, and garlic until chopped finely. With motor running, add oil in a thin, steady stream until dressing thickens.

preparation time 30 minutes
cooking time 20 minutes
serves 4

per serving 37.1g fat; 483 cal

bang bang chicken salad

Udon are Japanese noodles made from wheat flour.

1 pound boneless, skinless chicken thighs
7 ounces green beans, cut into 2-inch lengths
10½ ounces dried udon
3 cups baby tat soi, mizuna, or arugula
2 cups loosely packed fresh cilantro

SESAME AND PEANUT DRESSING
½ cup toasted sesame seeds
½ cup toasted unsalted peanuts
½ cup mirin
⅓ cup sake

1 Poach chicken, covered, in large pot of boiling water about 10 minutes or until cooked through. Cool chicken in liquid 10 minutes; slice thinly. Discard liquid.

2 Meanwhile, boil, steam, or microwave beans until tender; drain. Rinse under cold water; drain.

3 Blend or process ingredients for sesame and peanut dressing until combined.

4 Cook udon in large pot of boiling water, uncovered, until just tender; drain. Rinse under cold water; drain.

5 Place chicken, beans, and udon in large bowl with tat soi, cilantro, and dressing; toss gently to combine.

preparation time 20 minutes
cooking time 10 minutes
serves 4

per serving 29.6g fat; 689 cal

good old-fashioned chicken salad

1 quart (4 cups) boiling water
1 quart (4 cups) prepared chicken
   stock
1½ pounds boneless, skinless
   chicken breasts
1 long French baguette, sliced
   thinly
3 tablespoons olive oil
½ cup mayonnaise
½ cup sour cream
3 tablespoons lemon juice
4 trimmed celery stalks, sliced
   thinly
1 medium white onion, chopped
   finely
3 large dill pickles, sliced thinly
3 tablespoons finely chopped
   fresh flat-leaf parsley
1½ tablespoons finely chopped
   fresh tarragon
1 large head Boston or Bibb
   lettuce, leaves separated

1 Bring the water and stock to a
boil in large pot; poach chicken,
covered, about 10 minutes or until
cooked through. Cool chicken
in liquid 10 minutes; slice thinly.
Discard liquid.
2 Meanwhile, brush both sides of
bread slices with oil; toast under
preheated broiler until browned
lightly on both sides.
3 Whisk mayonnaise, sour
cream, and lemon juice in small
bowl. Combine chicken with
celery, onion, pickles, and herbs
in large bowl; toss gently to
combine. Place lettuce leaves on
serving platter; top with salad and
bread, drizzle with mayonnaise
mixture.

preparation time 40 minutes
cooking time 15 minutes
serves 4

per serving 41.1g fat; 794 cal

tips
Use whole-egg mayonnaise in this
recipe.

Cooling chicken in liquid prevents
the chicken from drying out.

chicken caesar salad

The original Caesar salad was created in Tijuana, Mexico, sometime during the 1920s in a restaurant owned by one Caesar Cardini. Since that time, it has been transformed into myriad individual interpretations by chefs around the world, and ours is a case in point: it took us weeks of development to come up with a version that everyone in the test kitchen agreed was perfect.

1 long French baguette
½ cup olive oil
2 cloves garlic, crushed
1¼ pounds boneless, skinless chicken breasts
7 slices bacon (10 ounces)
1 large head romaine lettuce, trimmed, torn
6 green onions, sliced thinly
¼ cup coarsely chopped fresh flat-leaf parsley
3½ ounces parmesan cheese, shaved

CAESAR DRESSING
1 egg
1 clove garlic, quartered
3 tablespoons lemon juice
1 teaspoon Dijon mustard
6 drained anchovy fillets
¾ cup olive oil
1½ tablespoons hot water, approximately

1 Preheat oven to 350. Make Caesar dressing.

2 Halve bread lengthwise; slice halves on the diagonal into ½-inch-thick slices. Combine oil and garlic in large bowl; add bread, toss to coat in oil mixture. Place bread, in single layer, on baking sheets; toast about 10 minutes or until croutons are browned lightly.

3 Meanwhile, cook chicken, in batches, on heated oiled grill or grill pan until browned on both sides and cooked through. Cook bacon on same grill pan until browned and crisp; drain on paper towels. Slice chicken thinly; slice bacon thinly.

4 Combine half of the chicken, half of the bacon, half of the croutons, and half of the dressing in large bowl with lettuce, half of the onion, half of the parsley, and half of the cheese; toss gently to combine.

5 Divide salad among serving bowls; top with remaining chicken, bacon, croutons, onions, parsley, and cheese. Drizzle with remaining dressing.

caesar dressing Blend or process egg, garlic, lemon juice, mustard, and anchovies until smooth. With motor running, add oil in a thin, steady stream until dressing thickens. If thinner dressing is preferred, stir in as much of the water as desired.

preparation time 20 minutes
cooking time 35 minutes
serves 4

per serving 88.5g fat; 1220 cal

tip
Caesar dressing and croutons can be prepared a day ahead. Cover and refrigerate dressing; store croutons in airtight container.

chicken and rice salad with nam jim dressing

Like most Thai sauces and dressings, nam jim is extremely hot. Seed the chilies to lessen the heat, if you prefer.

1 quart (4 cups) water
1¼ pounds boneless, skinless chicken breasts
6-inch piece fresh lemongrass
2 star anise
¾-inch piece fresh ginger, sliced thickly
1½ tablespoons peanut oil
1 small onion, chopped finely
1 cup basmati and wild rice mix
10½ ounces snow peas, trimmed
1 medium yellow bell pepper, sliced thinly
5 cups mizuna, arugula, or young mustard greens
½ cup firmly packed fresh cilantro

NAM JIM DRESSING
4-inch piece fresh lemongrass, chopped coarsely
2 cloves garlic, quartered
2 long green chilies, chopped coarsely
3 tablespoons lime juice
3 tablespoons peanut oil
1½ tablespoons brown sugar
1½ tablespoons fish sauce

1 Bring the water to a boil in medium pot; poach chicken, lemongrass, star anise, and ginger, covered, about 10 minutes or until chicken is cooked through. Cool chicken in liquid 10 minutes. Strain and reserve cooking liquid; discard lemongrass, star anise, and ginger. Slice chicken thinly.

2 Meanwhile, blend or process ingredients for nam jim dressing until smooth.

3 Heat oil in same cleaned pot; cook onion, stirring, until soft. Add rice; cook, stirring, 1 minute. Add reserved cooking liquid; bring to a boil. Reduce heat; simmer, uncovered, about 15 minutes or until rice is just tender. Drain; cool 10 minutes.

4 Meanwhile, boil, steam, or microwave snow peas until just tender; drain. Rinse under cold water; drain.

5 Place chicken, rice, and snow peas in large bowl with bell pepper, greens, cilantro, and dressing; toss gently to combine.

preparation time 20 minutes
cooking time 35 minutes
serves 4

per serving 17.6g fat; 519 cal

tips
You can use a rotisserie chicken for this recipe; however, you must cook the rice in a mixture of water and prepared chicken stock instead of using the cooking liquid.

You can find lemongrass at Asian markets; buy it fresh.

chicken, sweet potato and arugula salad with pecan salsa

12 chicken tenders (2 pounds)
3 tablespoons olive oil
2 cloves garlic, crushed
1½ tablespoons finely grated lemon peel
1½ tablespoons lemon juice
2 teaspoons hot paprika
1 large sweet potato (about 1 pound), sliced thinly
5 cups baby arugula

PECAN SALSA
1 cup coarsely chopped toasted pecans
2 small tomatoes, seeded, chopped finely
1 medium red onion, chopped finely
½ cup coarsely chopped fresh flat-leaf parsley
⅓ cup olive oil
¼ cup balsamic vinegar
1 clove garlic, crushed
2 teaspoons finely grated lemon peel

1 Combine chicken, oil, garlic, lemon peel, lemon juice, and paprika in large bowl, cover; refrigerate 2 hours.

2 Meanwhile, make pecan salsa.

3 Cook sliced sweet potato, in batches, on heated oiled grill or grill pan until browned on both sides and just tender.

4 Drain chicken; discard marinade. Cook chicken, in batches, on same grill or pan until browned and cooked through. Cover; let stand 5 minutes. Slice chicken thickly.

5 Serve sweet potato, arugula, and chicken with salsa.

pecan salsa Combine nuts, tomatoes, onion, and parsley in medium bowl. Whisk remaining ingredients in small bowl until dressing is combined. Stir dressing into nut mixture.

preparation time 25 minutes (plus refrigeration time)
cooking time 20 minutes
serves 4

per serving 55.4g fat; 805 cal

tip
Sweet potato may be replaced with pumpkin or butternut squash, and baby arugula replaced with baby spinach, if desired.

chicken sausage and couscous salad

Preserved lemons, a dominant ingredient in North African cooking, are salted lemons bottled for several months; the flavor is distinctively perfumed. To use, rinse well, discard flesh, using peel only.

8 thick chicken sausages
    (1¼ pounds)
1½ cups prepared chicken stock
1½ cups couscous
⅓ cup finely chopped preserved
    lemon peel
1 medium red bell pepper, sliced
    thinly
10½-ounce can chickpeas,
    rinsed, drained
1 cup pitted large green olives,
    halved lengthwise
1 cup loosely packed fresh
    cilantro
1 small white onion, sliced thinly
⅓ cup lemon juice
⅓ cup olive oil

1 Cook sausages on heated oiled grill or grill pan until browned and cooked through; drain on paper towels. Slice thinly.

2 Meanwhile, bring stock to a boil in medium pot. Remove from heat; stir in couscous. Cover; let stand about 5 minutes or until stock is absorbed, fluffing with fork occasionally.

3 Place sausages and couscous in large bowl with remaining ingredients; toss gently to combine.

preparation time 25 minutes
cooking time 15 minutes
serves 4

per serving 57.2g fat; 983 cal

tip
Preserved lemons can be difficult to find; to make your own, cut several slits in a lemon and fill with salt. Wrap the lemon in plastic wrap and refrigerate at least 24 hours.

chili quail, tangerine and grape salad

8 whole quails (3½ pounds)
4 fresh small red serrano or Thai chilies, chopped coarsely
2 cloves garlic, halved
¼ cup olive oil
3 tablespoons lemon juice
4 medium tangerines (about 1¾ pounds)
10½ ounces snow peas, trimmed, halved
12 ounces watercress, trimmed
1 cup toasted blanched almonds
7 ounces seedless red grapes, halved lengthwise

1 Using kitchen scissors, cut along both sides of each quail's backbone; discard backbones. Place each quail flat, skin-side down, on chopping board; discard ribcages. Cut each quail into quarters.

2 Blend or process chilies, garlic, oil, and half of the lemon juice until smooth; combine with quail pieces in large bowl. Cover; refrigerate 20 minutes.

3 Meanwhile, segment peeled tangerines over large bowl to save juice. Reserve segments with juice.

4 Cook undrained quail on heated oiled grill or grill pan until browned on both sides and cooked through.

5 Meanwhile, boil, steam, or microwave peas until just tender; drain.

6 Place quail and peas in large bowl with tangerine segments and juice, watercress, nuts, grapes, and remaining lemon juice; toss gently to combine.

preparation time 40 minutes (plus refrigeration time)
cooking time 20 minutes
serves 4

per serving 62.4g fat; 889 cal

tips
You can also cook the quail for about 15 minutes, if you prefer.

Boned quails can often be pre-ordered from your butcher.

mixed pea, fava bean and turkey salad with whole-grain mustard dressing

2½-pound single turkey breast
1½ tablespoons olive oil
1½ tablespoons sea salt
½ teaspoon freshly ground black pepper
2 teaspoons finely grated lemon peel
1½ cups risoni
1¾ pounds fresh fava beans
1¾ cups shelled fresh peas
10½ ounces sugar snap peas, trimmed
7 ounces snow peas, trimmed
¼ cup coarsely chopped fresh mint
7 ounces mung bean sprouts
2 cups baby arugula

LEMON MUSTARD DRESSING
3 tablespoons lemon juice
2 teaspoons whole-grain mustard
3 tablespoons white wine vinegar
1 teaspoon sugar
⅓ cup olive oil

1 Preheat oven to 400.

2 Tie turkey breast at 2½-inch intervals with kitchen string. Place on oiled baking sheet; rub with combined oil, salt, pepper, and lemon peel. Cover with aluminum foil; bake 40 minutes. Remove aluminum foil; bake about 10 minutes or until cooked through.

3 Meanwhile, whisk together ingredients for lemon mustard dressing.

4 Cook risoni in large pot of boiling water, uncovered, until just tender; drain. Rinse under cold water; drain.

5 Shell fava beans; discard pods. Boil, steam, or microwave beans until just tender; drain. Rinse under cold water; drain. Peel away gray-colored outer shells.

6 Meanwhile, boil, steam, or microwave all peas, together, until just tender; drain. Rinse under cold water; drain.

7 Place risoni, beans, and pea mixture in large bowl with mint, sprouts, arugula, and dressing; toss gently to combine. Slice turkey thinly; top salad with turkey.

preparation time 1 hour 15 minutes
cooking time 50 minutes
serves 6

per serving 35.2g fat; 1011 cal

tip
You can use a 1-pound package of frozen fava beans for this recipe. After thawing, peel away the gray outer shell then boil, steam, or microwave the inner bean until just tender.

warm duck, orange and mushroom salad

3 tablespoons honey
¼ cup orange juice
3 tablespoons soy sauce
1 clove garlic, crushed
4 duck breast fillets (1¼ pounds)
10½ ounces oyster mushrooms
7 ounces button mushrooms,
  sliced thickly
10½ ounces shiitake mushrooms,
  halved
3 large oranges (about 2 pounds),
  segmented
3½ ounces Bibb or Boston
  lettuce leaves

1 Preheat oven to 400.

2 Combine honey, orange juice, soy sauce, and garlic in small bowl. Score each piece of duck shallowly; brush with about ¼ cup of the honey mixture.

3 Combine mushrooms with remaining honey mixture in large broiler-safe roasting pan. Place duck on wire rack over pan; roast, uncovered, 10 minutes.

4 Remove duck and wire rack from dish; drain mushrooms, reserving about a third of the pan juices. Place mushrooms in large bowl.

5 Replace duck on wire rack over same pan; brown under preheated broiler until skin crisps. Slice duck thickly.

6 Add oranges, lettuce, and reserved pan juices to mushrooms; toss gently to combine. Divide salad among serving plates, then top with duck slices.

preparation time 25 minutes
cooking time 15 minutes
serves 4

per serving 9g fat; 338 cal

grilled turkey kebabs with endive and grapefruit salad

Dark-red dried barberries, slightly tart in flavor and elongated in shape, can be found in Middle Eastern and specialty food stores, sometimes sold as zereshk.

1¾ pounds turkey breast steaks, diced into ¾-inch pieces
3 tablespoons olive oil
1 clove garlic, crushed
3 small pink grapefruits (about 2 pounds)
4 white Belgian endives (about 1 pound)
2 trimmed celery stalks, sliced thinly
2 cups loosely packed fresh flat-leaf parsley
1 medium red onion, sliced thinly
3 tablespoons dried barberries
¼ cup toasted shelled pistachios, chopped coarsely

CITRUS DRESSING
¼ cup olive oil
1½ tablespoons lime juice
2 teaspoons sugar

1 Thread turkey onto skewers; brush with combined oil and garlic. Cover; refrigerate until needed.
2 Segment peeled grapefruits over small bowl to save juice; reserve segments and juice separately.
3 Separate endive leaves; combine in large bowl with grapefruit segments, celery, parsley, onion, and barberries. Make citrus dressing.
4 Cook turkey skewers on heated oiled grill or grill pan until browned and cooked through.
5 Add dressing and nuts to salad; toss gently to combine. Serve salad with turkey skewers.

citrus dressing Strain reserved grapefruit juice into measuring cup; whisk together with oil, lime juice, and sugar.

preparation time 40 minutes
cooking time 15 minutes
serves 4

per serving 34.3g fat; 562 cal

tip
You need 12 small bamboo skewers for this recipe; soak them in cold water for at least an hour before use to avoid splintering or scorching.

meat

Tasty beef, lamb, and pork cuts, prepared and cooked in a variety of ways, add substance to a salad, especially when drizzled with a tantalizing dressing.

beef salad with fresh rice noodles

1¼ pounds beef fillet, trimmed, sliced thinly
1½ tablespoons peanut oil
2 pounds fresh rice noodles
1 cup finely shredded Chinese cabbage
1 cup finely shredded red cabbage
½ cup loosely packed fresh basil
½ cup loosely packed fresh mint
½ cup loosely packed fresh cilantro
6 green onions, sliced thinly

CHILI SOY DRESSING
¼ cup sweet Thai chili sauce
¼ cup soy sauce
3 tablespoons lime juice
3 tablespoons peanut oil
2 fresh small red serrano or Thai chilies, seeded, sliced thinly
1½ tablespoons finely chopped fresh lemongrass
¾-inch piece fresh ginger, grated

1 Whisk together ingredients for chili soy dressing.
2 Combine beef in medium bowl with a third of the dressing, cover; refrigerate 3 hours or overnight.
3 Heat oil in wok or large skillet; stir-fry beef, in batches, until browned.
4 Place noodles in large heatproof bowl; cover with boiling water, separate with fork, drain. Rinse noodles under cold water; drain.
5 Place beef in large bowl with cabbages, herbs, onions, and remaining dressing; toss gently to combine. Divide noodles among serving bowls; top with beef salad.

preparation time 25 minutes (plus refrigeration time)
cooking time 15 minutes
serves 4

per serving 20.9g fat; 588 cal

potato, beet and pastrami salad with horseradish mayonnaise

1½ pounds tiny new potatoes, halved
7 trimmed red radishes
8 ounces red leaf lettuce, trimmed
10½ ounces pastrami, torn into large pieces
12 gherkin pickles, drained, halved lengthwise
3 tablespoons coarsely chopped fresh dill
1½ tablespoons olive oil
1½ tablespoons red wine vinegar
3 medium fresh beets (about 1 pound), peeled, grated coarsely

HORSERADISH MAYONNAISE
1 egg
1½ tablespoons prepared horseradish
1½ tablespoons lemon juice
½ cup olive oil

1 Boil, steam, or microwave potatoes until just tender; drain. Cool 10 minutes.

2 Meanwhile, make horseradish mayonnaise.

3 Slice radishes thinly; cut slices into thin strips. Combine potatoes and radishes in large bowl with lettuce, pastrami, gherkins, and dill. Combine oil, vinegar, and beets in medium bowl.

4 Divide pastrami salad among serving plates; top with beet salad, drizzle with mayonnaise.

horseradish mayonnaise Blend or process egg, horseradish, and lemon juice until combined. With motor running, add oil in a thin, steady stream until mayonnaise thickens slightly.

preparation time 30 minutes
cooking time 10 minutes
serves 4

per serving 39.8g fat; 582 cal

beef carpaccio with arugula, parmesan and aïoli

Carpaccio is to the Italians as sashimi is to the Japanese. Usually served as an appetizer, this delicately sliced raw beef fillet is usually served drizzled with olive oil and lemon juice.

14 ounces piece beef fillet, trimmed
3 cups arugula
3½ ounces parmesan cheese, shaved

AÏOLI
1 egg
1 clove garlic, quartered
1½ tablespoons lemon juice
1½ tablespoons Dijon mustard
½ cup olive oil

1 Wrap beef tightly in plastic wrap; place in freezer about 1 hour or until partially frozen.
2 Meanwhile, make aïoli.
3 Using sharp knife, slice unwrapped beef as thinly as possible; divide beef among serving plates.
4 Top beef with arugula and cheese; drizzle with aïoli.

aïoli Blend or process egg, garlic, lemon juice, and mustard until combined. With motor running, add oil in a thin, steady stream until aïoli thickens slightly.

preparation time 20 minutes (plus freezing time)
serves 4

per serving 41.8g fat; 510 cal

thai beef and noodle salad

1¼ pounds piece beef fillet, trimmed
2 small cucumbers, seeded, sliced thinly
1 cup bean sprouts
1 medium red onion, sliced thinly
1 cup loosely packed fresh cilantro
1 cup loosely packed fresh mint
6 thin strips lime peel or
   1 tablespoon grated lime peel
vegetable oil, for deep-frying
7 ounces dried egg noodles

HOT AND SOUR DRESSING
⅓ cup lime juice
3 tablespoons fish sauce
1½ tablespoons brown sugar
1½ tablespoons finely sliced fresh lemongrass
3 fresh small red serrano or Thai chilies, sliced thinly
1 clove garlic, crushed

1 Whisk together ingredients for hot and sour dressing.

2 Cook beef on heated oiled grill or grill pan until browned and cooked as desired. Cover; let stand 10 minutes. Slice beef thinly.

3 Meanwhile, combine cucumbers, sprouts, onion, cilantro, mint, and lime peel in large bowl.

4 Heat oil in wok or large pot; deep-fry noodles, in batches, until puffed and browned lightly. Drain on paper towels.

5 Add beef and dressing to salad in bowl; toss gently to combine. Divide noodles among serving plates; top with beef salad.

preparation time 30 minutes
cooking time 30 minutes
serves 4

per serving 10.1g fat; 436 cal

tips
Dressing can be made a day ahead; cover and refrigerate.

Noodles can be deep-fried a day ahead; store in an airtight container.

gremolata lamb salad

Italian gremolata, a mixture of finely chopped parsley, lemon peel, and garlic, is traditionally an accompaniment for osso buco, but it tastes perfect here.

8 ounces farfalle
1¼ pounds asparagus, trimmed, halved crosswise
7 ounces green beans, trimmed, halved crosswise
1½ tablespoons vegetable oil
1¾ pounds eye of lamb loin
2 teaspoons Dijon mustard
3 shallots, sliced thinly
⅓ cup toasted pine nuts
⅓ cup loosely packed fresh flat-leaf parsley

LEMON DIJON DRESSING
3 tablespoons lemon juice
3 tablespoons extra virgin olive oil
2 teaspoons Dijon mustard

GREMOLATA
2 cloves garlic, chopped finely
1½ tablespoons finely grated lemon peel
½ cup finely chopped fresh flat-leaf parsley

1 Whisk together ingredients for lemon Dijon dressing. Combine ingredients for gremolata in small bowl.

2 Cook pasta in large pot of boiling water, uncovered, until just tender; drain. Rinse under cold water; drain.

3 Meanwhile, boil, steam, or microwave asparagus and beans, separately, until just tender; drain.

4 Heat oil in large skillet; cook lamb, uncovered, until browned and cooked as desired. Spread lamb with mustard; press gremolata firmly onto mustard on lamb. Cover; let stand 5 minutes. Slice lamb thickly.

5 Place pasta, asparagus, beans, and lamb in large bowl with shallots, pine nuts, parsley, and dressing; toss gently to combine.

preparation time 20 minutes
cooking time 20 minutes
serves 4

per serving 30.7g fat; 694 cal

tip
Farfalle, also called butterflies or bowties, is a short, solid pasta that stands up well to being tossed in a salad. Try not to overcook the pasta; it should be al dente.

lamb, bulgur and grilled zucchini salad

1¼ pounds lamb fillets, trimmed
3 tablespoons olive oil
1 clove garlic, crushed
1½ tablespoons coarsely chopped fresh sage
3 tablespoons coarsely chopped fresh oregano
1½ cups bulgur wheat
2 teaspoons finely grated lemon peel
¼ cup loosely packed fresh oregano
2 medium yellow squash
2 medium green zucchini
8 ounces yellow grape tomatoes, halved
8 ounces cherry tomatoes, halved
1 cup firmly packed fresh flat-leaf parsley

LEMON GARLIC DRESSING
3 tablespoons lemon juice
1 clove garlic, crushed
¼ cup olive oil

1 Combine lamb, oil, garlic, sage, and chopped oregano in large bowl, cover; refrigerate 3 hours or overnight.
2 Place bulgur wheat in medium bowl; cover with cold water. Let stand 10 minutes; drain. Squeeze out as much excess water by hand as possible. Spread bulgur wheat in a thin, even layer on tray; let stand 15 minutes. Return dry bulgur wheat to same bowl with peel and oregano leaves; toss gently to combine.
3 Meanwhile, whisk together ingredients for lemon garlic dressing.
4 Cook lamb on heated oiled grill or grill pan until browned and cooked as desired. Cover; let stand 10 minutes. Slice lamb thickly.
5 Meanwhile, using sharp knife, v-slicer, or mandoline, cut zucchini into ribbons; cook zucchini, in batches, on same cleaned heated oiled grill or pan until just tender. Combine zucchini in medium bowl with tomatoes, parsley, and half of the dressing.
6 Add remaining dressing to bulgur wheat mixture; toss gently to combine. Divide bulgur wheat mixture among serving plates; top with zucchini mixture, then lamb pieces.

preparation time 45 minutes (plus refrigeration and standing times)
cooking time 20 minutes
serves 4

per serving 29.2g fat; 510 cal

tips
Let the cooked lamb rest, covered, for 10 minutes before slicing to allow the juices to settle; drain away any accumulated juice from the meat platter before slicing the lamb. This helps prevent the bulgur wheat from becoming soggy.

This salad can be served warm or cold.

merguez, beet and lentil salad

Merguez sausages, from North Africa, are traditionally made with lamb and seasoned with garlic and hot spices. They can be found at delicatessens and sausage specialists. Golden beets have a slightly sweeter flavor than the purple-red variety, but if you can't find them, red beets will do nicely. When trimming the beets, leave a little of the stalk intact to prevent bleeding during cooking.

2 cups brown lentils
2 sprigs fresh thyme
20 baby red beets (about
    1 pound)
20 baby golden beets (about
    1 pound)
8 merguez sausages (1¼ pounds)
1 large onion, chopped finely
2 teaspoons mustard seeds
2 teaspoons ground cumin
1 teaspoon ground coriander
½ cup prepared chicken stock
10½ cups spinach, trimmed,
    chopped coarsely

THYME DRESSING

1 teaspoon finely chopped fresh
    thyme
1 clove garlic, crushed
½ cup red wine vinegar
¼ cup extra virgin olive oil

1 Whisk together ingredients for thyme dressing.

2 Cook lentils with thyme sprigs, uncovered, in large pot of boiling water until tender; drain lentils, discard thyme sprigs. Place lentils in large bowl with half of the dressing; toss gently to combine.

3 Meanwhile, discard leaves and most of the stalk of each beet. Boil, steam, or microwave unpeeled beets until just tender; drain. When cool enough to handle, peel beets; cut each beet in half.

4 Cook sausages in large, heated non-stick skillet until browned and cooked through. Cool 5 minutes; slice thickly.

5 Reheat same skillet; cook onion, mustard seeds, cumin, and coriander, stirring, until onion softens. Add stock; bring to a boil. Remove from heat; stir in spinach.

6 Add spinach mixture, beets, sausages, and remaining dressing to lentil mixture; toss gently to combine.

preparation time 30 minutes
cooking time 50 minutes
serves 4

per serving 45.2g fat; 948 cal

greek lamb salad

Skordalia is a pungent Greek sauce or dip made with bread (or sometimes potatoes), garlic, lemon juice, and olive oil. It can be served with almost any kind of dish—from grilled meats and poultry to fish and raw vegetables.

1¼ pounds lamb tenderloin, trimmed
3 tablespoons olive oil
2 teaspoons finely grated lemon peel
1 teaspoon finely chopped fresh marjoram
1 clove garlic, crushed
1 large green bell pepper, sliced thinly
1 cucumber, diced into ¾-inch pieces
14 ounces grape tomatoes, halved
2 trimmed celery stalks, sliced thinly
4 green onions, sliced thinly
2 heads baby romaine lettuce, chopped coarsely
1 cup pitted kalamata olives
7 ounces goat feta, crumbled

SKORDALIA
2 slices stale white bread
2 cloves garlic, crushed
3 tablespoons olive oil
2 teaspoons white wine vinegar
1½ tablespoons lemon juice
⅓ cup water

MARJORAM DRESSING
3 tablespoons olive oil
3 tablespoons white wine vinegar
1½ tablespoons finely chopped fresh marjoram
pinch cayenne pepper

1 Place lamb, oil, lemon peel, marjoram, and garlic in large bowl; toss to coat lamb. Cover; refrigerate 1 hour.

2 Meanwhile, make skordalia. Whisk together ingredients for marjoram dressing.

3 Heat large non-stick skillet; cook lamb, in batches, until browned and cooked as desired. Cover; let stand 5 minutes. Slice lamb thickly.

4 Place lamb in large bowl with remaining ingredients and dressing; toss gently to combine. Divide salad among serving plates; drizzle with skordalia.

skordalia Discard crusts from bread, soak in small bowl of cold water; drain. Squeeze out excess water; blend or process bread and remaining ingredients until mixture is smooth.

preparation time 40 minutes (plus refrigeration time)
cooking time 10 minutes
serves 4

per serving 46.1g fat; 710 cal

za'atar lamb with warm chickpea salad

1 cup dried chickpeas
1 bay leaf
1¾ pounds eye of lamb loin
¼ cup olive oil
1½ tablespoons sumac
1½ tablespoons toasted sesame
  seeds
1 teaspoon dried thyme
1 teaspoon dried oregano
1 teaspoon dried marjoram
1 teaspoon sweet paprika
1½ tablespoons butter
12 baby onions, halved
2 large carrots, chopped finely
2 trimmed celery stalks, chopped
  finely
2 small fennel bulbs, trimmed,
  sliced thinly
1 cup firmly packed fresh flat-leaf
  parsley

SUMAC DRESSING

1½ tablespoons sumac
1 teaspoon Dijon mustard
¼ cup olive oil
¼ cup lemon juice

1 Place chickpeas in large bowl of cold water; let stand overnight. Drain.

2 Cook chickpeas and bay leaf in medium pot of boiling water, uncovered, until just tender; drain. Rinse under cold water; drain.

3 Meanwhile, place lamb, 3 tablespoons of the oil, and combined sumac, sesame seeds, dried herbs, and paprika in large bowl; toss to coat lamb. Cover; refrigerate 30 minutes.

4 Whisk together ingredients for sumac dressing.

5 Heat butter and remaining oil in large skillet; cook onions, stirring, about 10 minutes or until browned lightly and softened. Add carrots, celery, and fennel; cook, stirring, until vegetables are just tender.

6 Meanwhile, cook lamb, in batches, on heated oiled grill or grill pan until browned and cooked as desired. Cover; let stand 5 minutes. Slice lamb thickly.

7 Just before serving, combine chickpeas, parsley, and half of the dressing with vegetables; cook, stirring, until heated through. Divide chickpea salad among serving plates; top with lamb, drizzle with remaining dressing.

preparation time 45 minutes (plus standing and refrigeration times)
cooking time 40 minutes
serves 4

per serving 47.9g fat; 763 cal

tips
Za'atar, a mixture of toasted sesame seeds, dried marjoram, thyme, and sumac, can be found already blended in Middle Eastern food stores. Alternatively, you can make your own blend, as we have here.

Sumac, a purple-red, very astringent spice, adds a tart, lemony flavor to dips and dressings and goes well with barbecued meats. It, too, can be found in Middle Eastern markets.

lamb cutlets and black-eyed pea salad

12 lamb rib chops (2 pounds)
2 teaspoons ground coriander
½ teaspoon cayenne pepper
2 teaspoons smoked paprika
1½ tablespoons vegetable oil
1½ cups dried black-eyed peas
10 baby vine-ripened tomatoes,
    quartered
2 trimmed celery stalks, sliced
    thinly
1 small head red leaf lettuce,
    trimmed
3 tablespoons lemon juice

PARSLEY DRESSING
3 tablespoons coarsely chopped,
    fresh flat-leaf parsley
1½ tablespoons whole-grain
    mustard
1 clove garlic, crushed
¼ cup extra virgin olive oil
¼ cup white wine vinegar

1 Combine lamb, coriander, pepper, paprika, and oil in large bowl. Cover; refrigerate 3 hours or overnight.

2 Cook beans in medium pot of boiling water, uncovered, about 30 minutes or until just tender.

3 Meanwhile, cook lamb, in batches, on heated oiled grill or grill pan until browned on both sides and cooked as desired.

4 Whisk together ingredients for parsley dressing. Place drained beans in large bowl with tomatoes, celery, and dressing; toss gently to combine.

5 Divide lettuce leaves among serving plates; top with bean salad then lamb; drizzle with lemon juice.

preparation time 20 minutes (plus refrigeration time)
cooking time 35 minutes
serves 4

per serving 33.5g fat; 562 cal

crisp spicy pancetta and roasted potato salad

3½ pounds tiny new potatoes, halved
3 tablespoons olive oil
14 ounces hot pancetta
15 small vine-ripened tomatoes (about 1 pound), seeded, chopped coarsely
1 cup pitted marinated black olives
5 cups arugula

PARMESAN AND BASIL DRESSING
¼ cup toasted pine nuts
¼ cup coarsely grated parmesan cheese
¾ cup loosely packed fresh basil
1 clove garlic, quartered
⅓ cup olive oil

1 Preheat oven to 425.
2 Place combined potatoes and oil on baking sheet. Roast, uncovered, about 30 minutes or until browned lightly, and tender.
3 Meanwhile, blend or process ingredients for parmesan and basil dressing until just combined.
4 Cook pancetta, in batches, in heated large non-stick skillet until crisp; drain on paper towels.
5 Combine potatoes and half of the dressing in large bowl; add pancetta, tomatoes, olives, and arugula. Toss salad gently to combine; divide among serving plates, then drizzle with remaining salad dressing.

preparation time 20 minutes
cooking time 35 minutes
serves 4

per serving 50.8g fat; 841 cal

pork, coconut, lime and tofu salad

2 pounds pork fillets, trimmed
1½ tablespoons vegetable oil
3 tablespoons lime juice
1¼ pounds baby bok choy, quartered
2 large carrots
8 ounces fried tofu pieces
½ cup coarsely chopped fresh basil
½ cup coarsely chopped fresh cilantro
1¼ cups bean sprouts
4 green onions, sliced thinly
¼ cup shredded coconut

COCONUT DRESSING
3 tablespoons lime juice
1½ tablespoons fish sauce
1½ tablespoons sweet Thai chili sauce
1 fresh small red serrano or Thai chili, seeded, sliced thinly
¾ cup coconut milk

1 Whisk together ingredients for coconut dressing.

2 Place pork, oil, and lime juice in medium bowl; toss to coat pork. Cook pork on heated oiled grill or grill pan until browned and cooked as desired. Cover; let stand 5 minutes. Slice pork thinly.

3 Meanwhile, boil, steam, or microwave bok choy until just wilted; drain.

4 Cut carrots into 3-inch pieces. Using sharp knife, mandoline, or v-slicer, cut pieces lengthwise into thin slices; cut slices into matchstick-sized pieces.

5 Place pork, bok choy, and carrots in large bowl with dressing and remaining ingredients; toss gently to combine.

preparation time 40 minutes
cooking time 10 minutes
serves 4

per serving 24.4g fat; 521 cal

hazelnut pork salad

1¼ pounds pork fillets, trimmed
10½ ounces dried udon
3½ cups baby arugula
4 ounces baby curly endive leaves
½ cup toasted hazelnuts,
    chopped coarsely

HAZELNUT DRESSING
3 tablespoons peanut oil
2 cloves garlic, crushed
½-inch piece fresh ginger, grated
1½ tablespoons hazelnut oil
⅓ cup brown rice vinegar

1 Cook pork on heated, oiled grill pan until browned and cooked as desired. Cover; let stand about 5 minutes. Slice pork thinly.

2 Meanwhile, cook udon in large pot of boiling water, uncovered, until just tender; drain. Rinse under cold water; drain.

3 Whisk together ingredients for hazelnut dressing.

4 Place pork in large bowl with dressing and remaining ingredients; toss gently to combine. Divide noodles among serving plates; top with salad.

preparation time 20 minutes
cooking time 15 minutes
serves 4

per serving 29.1g fat; 675 cal

tip
Udon are Japanese noodles made from wheat flour. You can buy them at Asian food stores.

seafood

Crab, mussels, salmon, lobster, tuna, shrimp, and scallops all make stunning appearances in a variety of tempting salads on show in this section.

barbecued seafood and green mango salad

1 pound uncooked medium
  shrimp
8 ounces cleaned calamari
1 pound cleaned baby octopus,
  halved lengthwise
1 large green mango (about
  1¼ pounds)
7 cups mizuna, arugula, or young
  mustard greens
8 ounces cherry tomatoes, halved
3½ ounces mung bean sprouts
1 cup loosely packed fresh mint

LEMONGRASS DRESSING

2 fresh small red serrano or Thai
  chilies, seeded, chopped finely
3 tablespoons fish sauce
1½ tablespoons brown sugar
⅓ cup peanut oil
¼ cup finely chopped fresh
  lemongrass
¼ cup lime juice

1 Whisk together ingredients for lemongrass dressing.
2 Peel and devein shrimp, leaving tails intact. Combine calamari and shrimp in large bowl with octopus and half of the dressing, cover; refrigerate 2 hours.
3 Meanwhile, slice mango thinly; cut slices into matchstick-sized pieces.
4 Cook seafood, in batches, on heated oiled grill or grill pan until browned and cooked as desired.
5 Combine seafood and mango in large bowl with remaining dressing and remaining ingredients; toss gently to combine.

preparation time 40 minutes
(plus refrigeration time)
cooking time 15 minutes
serves 4

per serving 22g fat; 550 cal

hot and sour shrimp vermicelli salad

2 pounds cooked medium shrimp
8 ounces rice vermicelli
1 lime
1 lemon
1 medium red bell pepper, sliced thinly
1 medium yellow bell pepper, sliced thinly
1 medium red onion, sliced thinly
¼ cup olive oil
¼ cup rice vinegar
1½ tablespoons sambal oelek
1½ tablespoons fish sauce
3 tablespoons brown sugar
1 cup firmly packed fresh cilantro

1 Peel and devein shrimp, leaving tails intact. Place vermicelli in large heatproof bowl of boiling water, let stand until just tender; drain. Rinse under cold water; drain well.

2 Meanwhile, halve lime and lemon lengthwise; slice 1 unpeeled half of each thinly, place in large bowl. Squeeze remaining halves over bowl; add shrimp, vermicelli, and remaining ingredients, toss gently to combine. Cover; refrigerate 1 hour before serving.

preparation time 30 minutes (plus refrigeration time)
serves 4

per serving 14.9g fat; 359 cal

tip
Sambal oelek is a hot chili paste that can be found in Asian markets, or you can substitute with a chili paste of your choosing.

crab pasta salad with warm tomato, tarragon and basil sauce

10 large plum tomatoes (about
  2 pounds)
1½ tablespoons sea salt
1 teaspoon cracked black pepper
⅓ cup olive oil
1 large onion, chopped finely
2 cloves garlic, crushed
1 cup white wine vinegar
2 cups loosely packed fresh basil
1 cup loosely packed fresh
  tarragon
6 cooked blue crabs (4½ pounds)
12 ounces linguine
10½ cups spinach, trimmed,
  chopped coarsely
3 tablespoons finely grated lemon
  peel

1 Preheat oven to 400.
2 Halve tomatoes; place, cut-side up, in single layer in large baking dish. Sprinkle tomatoes with combined salt, pepper, and 1½ tablespoons of the oil. Roast, uncovered, about 1 hour or until tomatoes soften and brown lightly.
3 Meanwhile, heat 1½ tablespoons of the remaining oil in medium pot; cook onion and garlic, stirring, until onion softens. Add vinegar; bring to a boil. Boil, uncovered, until mixture reduces by half.
4 Add tomatoes and remaining oil to pot, reduce heat; simmer, uncovered, 30 minutes. Stir in basil and tarragon; cook, uncovered, about 15 minutes or until mixture thickens slightly.
5 Meanwhile, holding crab firmly, slide sharp knife under top of shell at back; lever off shell. Discard whitish gills; rinse crab body under cold water then cut into quarters. Remove two large claws from each crab; using nut cracker or meat mallet, crack both sections of large claws, reserve. Remove flesh from body and remaining claws; flake into small pieces in large bowl.

6 Cook pasta in large pot of boiling water, uncovered, until tender. While pasta is cooking, strain tomato mixture through sieve, pressing firmly with wooden spoon, into bowl with crab. Discard solids left in sieve.
7 Add drained pasta, spinach, and lemon peel to bowl; toss gently to combine. Divide salad among serving bowls; top with reserved crab claws.

preparation time 30 minutes
cooking time 1 hour 55 minutes
serves 4

per serving 20.4g fat; 602 cal

ocean trout and asparagus salad with creamy horseradish dressing

4 small potatoes (about 1 pound), unpeeled
four 8-ounce ocean trout fillets, skin on
3 cups milk
3 cups water
1 pound asparagus, trimmed
6 ounces watercress, trimmed
1 small red onion, sliced thinly

CREAMY HORSERADISH DRESSING

1 egg
3 tablespoons prepared horseradish
2 teaspoons honey
⅔ cup olive oil

1 Boil, steam, or microwave potatoes until tender; drain. When cool enough to handle, slice thickly.

2 Meanwhile, remove any bones from fish. Place fish in large skillet; cover with milk and the water. Weigh fish down with heavy plate or lid to keep submerged; bring to a boil. Reduce heat; simmer, about 5 minutes or until fish is cooked as desired. Discard cooking liquid; when fish is cool enough to handle, remove skin, cut each fillet in half lengthwise.

3 Make creamy horseradish dressing.

4 Boil, steam, or microwave asparagus until tender; drain. Rinse under cold water; drain. Divide asparagus, watercress, onion, potatoes, and fish among serving plates; drizzle with dressing.

creamy horseradish dressing
Blend or process egg, horseradish, and honey until combined. With motor running, add oil in a thin, steady stream until dressing thickens slightly.

preparation time 30 minutes
cooking time 20 minutes
serves 4

per serving 53.7g fat; 836 cal

lobster and soba salad with ponzu dressing

Used extensively in Japanese cooking, daikon has a sweet, fresh flavor without the sharp bite of the more common red radish. Green tea soba are Japanese noodles made from buckwheat flour and green tea.

3 medium carrots
½ small daikon
4 green onions
7 ounces green tea soba noodles
4 cooked lobster tails
  (1½ pounds)
1 sheet toasted seaweed
  (yaki-nori), shredded finely

PONZU DRESSING
3 tablespoons mirin
3 tablespoons Japanese soy
  sauce
1 teaspoon sugar
1 teaspoon wasabi paste
½ teaspoon sesame oil

1 Using vegetable peeler, slice carrots and daikon into ribbons; cut ribbons in half lengthwise. Cut green onions into 4-inch lengths; cut each piece in half lengthwise. Place vegetables in large bowl of iced water; refrigerate 30 minutes.
2 Whisk together ingredients for ponzu dressing.
3 Cook soba in large pot of boiling water, uncovered, until just tender; drain. Rinse under cold water; drain well. Place soba in large bowl; add three-quarters of the dressing and toss gently.
4 Cut lobster tails in half lengthwise; remove vein. Divide drained vegetables among serving plates; top with soba and lobster tails, drizzle with remaining dressing, sprinkle with seaweed.

preparation time 25 minutes (plus refrigeration time)
cooking time 10 minutes
serves 4

per serving 2.7g fat; 337 cal

tips
Crab meat can be used instead of lobster.

The easiest way to shred nori without tearing the delicate sheets is to use kitchen scissors.

Green tea soba are available from most Asian food stores.

mussel and fava bean salad à la grecque

1 cup risoni
1 pound frozen fava beans
2 pounds medium mussels
½ cup water
½ cup dry white wine
7 ounces green beans, trimmed, cut into ¾-inch lengths
1 cup pitted kalamata olives
1 large red bell pepper, chopped coarsely

OREGANO AND RED WINE VINAIGRETTE
2 teaspoons finely chopped fresh oregano
3 tablespoons red wine vinegar
2 cloves garlic, crushed
1 small onion, grated finely
½ teaspoon ground cumin
⅓ cup extra virgin olive oil

1 Cook pasta and fava beans in separate medium pots of boiling water, uncovered, until each is just tender; drain. Cool separately about 10 minutes. Carefully peel away gray-colored outer shells of fava beans.

2 Meanwhile, scrub mussels; remove beards. Heat the water and wine in large pot. Add mussels; cook, covered, about 10 minutes or until mussels open (discard any that do not). Discard liquid. Reserve 16 mussels; cover to keep warm. Remove remaining mussels from shells; discard shells.

3 Whisk together ingredients for oregano and red wine vinaigrette.

4 Boil, steam, or microwave green beans until just tender; drain. Rinse under cold water; drain.

5 Combine pasta, fava beans, shelled mussels, and green beans in large bowl with olives, bell pepper, and vinaigrette; toss gently to combine. Divide salad among serving bowls; top with mussels in shells.

preparation time 30 minutes
cooking time 15 minutes
serves 4

per serving 20.6g fat; 549 cal

salmon pasta salad with lemon mayonnaise

Orecchiette is a bite-sized pasta, perfectly shaped to hold chunky vegetables in sauces or salads. It has a slightly different taste and texture to others, as it's made with a custom blend of durum wheat semolina.

8 ounces orecchiette
20 drained caperberries
two 14-ounce cans skinless, boneless red salmon, drained, flaked
1 large white onion, halved, sliced thinly
4 trimmed celery stalks, sliced thinly
4 large red cabbage leaves, trimmed

LEMON MAYONNAISE
3 tablespoons water
⅔ cup mayonnaise
½ cup sour cream
¼ cup lemon juice
¼ cup coarsely chopped fresh dill

1 Cook pasta in large pot of boiling water, uncovered, until just tender; drain. Rinse under cold water; drain.
2 Whisk ingredients for lemon mayonnaise in small bowl until well combined.
3 Slice eight of the caperberries thinly; combine in large bowl with salmon, onion, celery, pasta, and half of the mayonnaise; toss gently to combine. Divide cabbage among serving bowls; fill with salad, top with remaining mayonnaise and remaining caperberries.

preparation time 15 minutes
cooking time 10 minutes
serves 4

per serving 48.4g fat; 864 cal

tip
If you can't find orecchiette at your supermarket, try this recipe with fusilli.

tahitian fish salad

Often seen on menus as poisson cru, this delicious fish salad captures the tropical flavor of Tahitian cooking with every bite. Unlike that other popular "raw" fish dish, ceviche, where the seafood marinates in citrus juice for such a long time that it is virtually "cooked," here it is assembled quickly and submerged in lime juice only long enough to become slightly opaque on the surface, while remaining raw inside. The addition of the coconut milk, too, contributes to its particular Tahitian identity.

1¼-pound piece sea bass, skinned
⅔ cup lime juice
1 large sweet potato (about 1 pound), sliced thinly
1 hothouse cucumber
1½ tablespoons finely grated lime peel
3 fresh small red serrano or Thai chilies, sliced thinly
4 green onions, sliced thinly
1½ cups finely chopped cilantro leaf and stem mixture
1⅔ cups coconut milk
2 medium avocados (about 1 pound), sliced thinly

1 Slice fish in half lengthwise, remove bones; slice halves crosswise into ¼-inch strips. Combine fish with lime juice in large bowl, cover; refrigerate about 20 minutes.

2 Meanwhile, cook sweet potato on heated oiled grill or grill pan until browned lightly on both sides and just tender.

3 Using vegetable peeler, slice cucumber into ribbons. Add cucumber, lime peel, chilies, onions, cilantro, and coconut milk to undrained fish; toss gently to combine.

4 Divide sweet potato among serving plates, top with avocados and fish salad.

preparation time 40 minutes (plus refrigeration time)
cooking time 10 minutes
serves 4

per serving 44.2g fat; 636 cal

herbed and spiced sashimi with ginger cabbage salad

3 tablespoons sesame seeds
1½ tablespoons black sesame seeds
2 teaspoons coriander seeds
1 teaspoon sea salt
½ teaspoon cracked black pepper
3 tablespoons finely chopped fresh chives
10½-ounce piece sashimi tuna
10½-ounce piece sashimi salmon
7 ounces green beans, trimmed, sliced thinly
6 trimmed red radishes
3 cups finely shredded Chinese cabbage
6 green onions, sliced thinly
1½ cups mung bean sprouts
1 cup firmly packed fresh cilantro

GINGER DRESSING
¾-inch piece fresh ginger, grated
3 tablespoons rice vinegar
3 tablespoons vegetable oil
2 teaspoons sesame oil
1½ tablespoons mirin
1½ tablespoons soy sauce

1 Dry-fry seeds in small skillet, stirring, until fragrant; cool. Using mortar and pestle, crush seeds; combine in large bowl with salt, pepper and chives.
2 Cut each piece of fish into three 2-inch-thick pieces. Roll each piece in seed mixture; enclose tightly, individually, in plastic wrap. Refrigerate until needed.
3 Whisk together ingredients for ginger dressing.
4 Boil, steam, or microwave beans until just tender; drain. Rinse beans under cold water; drain. Slice radishes thinly; cut slices into matchstick-sized pieces.
5 Combine beans and radishes in large bowl with cabbage, onions, sprouts, cilantro, and half of the dressing; toss gently to combine.
6 Unwrap fish; slice thinly. Divide fish and salad among serving plates; drizzle fish with remaining dressing.

preparation time 45 minutes
cooking time 5 minutes
serves 4

per serving 26.1g fat; 409 cal

tip
Salmon and tuna sold as sashimi have to meet stringent guidelines regarding their handling and treatment after leaving the water; however, it is best to seek local advice from authorities before eating any raw fish.

chili-seared tuna with avocado cream, tortillas and grilled corn

Chipotle chilies are jalapeño chilies that have been dried and smoked, giving an intense, smoky flavor rather than a blast of heat.

4 chipotle chilies
1½ tablespoons olive oil
1 small onion, chopped finely
2 cloves garlic, crushed
⅓ cup loosely packed fresh oregano
3 tablespoons tomato paste
3 tablespoons water
four 7-ounce tuna steaks
2 ears fresh corn
   (about 1 pound), shucked
8 large flour tortillas
2 limes, cut into wedges

AVOCADO CREAM
2 small avocados
½ cup sour cream
¼ cup coarsely chopped fresh cilantro
1½ tablespoons lime juice

1 Place chilies in small heatproof bowl of boiling water; let stand 15 minutes. Drain; chop chilies coarsely.

2 Heat oil in small skillet; cook onion and garlic, stirring, until onion softens. Stir in chilies, oregano, paste, and the water; bring to a boil. Remove from heat; blend or process, pulsing, until mixture forms a thick paste.

3 Place fish, in single layer, in large shallow dish; using fingers, pat chili paste into both sides of fish. Cover; refrigerate 15 minutes.

4 Meanwhile, make avocado cream by blending or processing avocados and sour cream until smooth; stir in cilantro and lime juice.

5 Cook corn on heated oiled grill or grill pan until browned lightly and just tender; slice thickly, cover to keep warm. Cook undrained fish on same heated oiled grill or pan until browned on both sides and cooked as desired. Cover; let stand 5 minutes. Slice fish thickly.

6 Meanwhile, heat tortillas according to directions. Divide fish, corn, avocado cream, and tortillas among serving plates. Serve with lime wedges.

preparation time 30 minutes (plus standing and refrigeration times)
cooking time 25 minutes
serves 4

per serving 46.4g fat; 853 cal

tuna and white bean salad with vinaigrette

2 trimmed celery stalks
two 15-ounce cans tuna, drained, flaked
14-ounce can white beans, rinsed, drained
1 medium red onion, sliced thinly
1 cup pitted kalamata olives
1 medium red bell pepper, sliced thinly
1 cup firmly packed fresh flat-leaf parsley

VINAIGRETTE
1 clove garlic, crushed
⅓ cup lemon juice
⅓ cup olive oil

1 Whisk together ingredients for vinaigrette.
2 Cut celery into 2-inch pieces; cut pieces into thin strips lengthwise. Combine celery in large bowl with remaining ingredients.
3 Pour dressing over salad; toss gently to combine.

preparation time 15 minutes
serves 4

per serving 23g fat; 434 cal

tip
Many varieties of already cooked white beans are available canned, among them cannellini, butter, and haricot beans; any of these are suitable for this salad.

seared scallops with mixed cabbage salad

32 cleaned scallops (3 pounds)
2 small cucumbers
3 cups finely shredded red
    cabbage
2 cups finely shredded savoy
    cabbage
½ cup coarsely chopped fresh
    chives
3 tablespoons toasted sesame
    seeds

HONEY SOY DRESSING
3 tablespoons soy sauce
3 tablespoons lemon juice
2 teaspoons sesame oil
1½ tablespoons honey
1 clove garlic, crushed
¼ cup peanut oil

1 Whisk together ingredients for honey soy dressing.

2 Sear scallops in large heated oiled skillet, in batches, until browned on both sides and cooked as desired.

3 Using vegetable peeler, slice cucumbers into ribbons. Combine cucumber in large bowl with cabbages, chives, seeds, and three-quarters of the dressing.

4 Divide salad among serving plates; top with scallops, drizzle with remaining dressing.

preparation time 15 minutes
cooking time 10 minutes
serves 4

per serving 21g fat; 306 cal

shrimp, papaya and green apple salad

A fairly hard, unripe papaya is ideal for this recipe but if none is available, buy the firmest ripe papaya you can find. We used unpeeled granny smith apples in this recipe, both for their crisp tartness and pale green peel.

2 pounds cooked large shrimp
1 small daikon
2 small green apples, sliced thinly
1 medium red onion, sliced thinly
1 small papaya (about 1¼ pounds), diced into ½-inch pieces
1 small honeydew melon (about 2 pounds), diced into ½-inch pieces
14 ounces watercress, trimmed

WASABI DRESSING
3 tablespoons apple cider vinegar
1 teaspoon wasabi paste
1 clove garlic, crushed
1½ tablespoons lemon juice
¼ cup olive oil

1 Peel and devein shrimp, leaving tails intact.
2 Whisk together ingredients for wasabi dressing.
3 Slice daikon thinly; cut slices into matchstick-sized pieces. Place in large bowl with apples, onion, papaya, honeydew, and dressing; toss gently to combine. Divide watercress among serving plates; top with salad then shrimp.

preparation time 25 minutes
serves 4

per serving 15.3g fat; 365 cal

tips
This recipe should not be made until just before serving to avoid discoloration of the fruit.

Use a mandoline or v-slicer, if you own one or the other, to slice the daikon and apples as thinly as possible.

smoked seafood and mixed vegetable antipasti

⅓ cup sour cream
2 teaspoons raspberry vinegar
1½ tablespoons coarsely
  chopped fresh chives
1 clove garlic, crushed
1 large yellow squash
1½ tablespoons raspberry
  vinegar, extra
¼ cup extra virgin olive oil
⅓ cup toasted slivered almonds
1 cup drained sun-dried tomatoes
1 large avocado
1½ tablespoons lemon juice
10½ ounces smoked ocean trout
  or whitefish
7 ounces sliced smoked salmon
16 drained caperberries
1 lemon, cut into wedges
6-ounce package roasted garlic
  bagel chips

1 Combine sour cream, vinegar, chives, and garlic in small bowl, cover; refrigerate until needed.

2 Meanwhile, using vegetable peeler, slice squash lengthwise into ribbons; combine squash in small bowl with extra vinegar and 3 tablespoons of the oil.

3 Combine nuts, tomatoes, and remaining oil in small bowl. Slice avocado thickly into small bowl; sprinkle with juice. Flake trout into bite-sized pieces.

4 Arrange squash mixture, nut mixture, avocado, trout, salmon, and caperberries on large platter; serve with sour cream mixture, lemon, and bagel chips.

preparation time 35 minutes
serves 4

per serving 49.7g fat; 790 cal

sushi salad

2 cups sticky rice
2 cups water
2 small cucumbers
½ small daikon
1 lemon, unpeeled, quartered,
    sliced thinly
14-ounce piece sashimi salmon,
    sliced thinly
¼ cup toasted sesame seeds
1 sheet toasted seaweed
    (yaki-nori), shredded finely

MIRIN AND WASABI DRESSING

1½-inch piece fresh ginger, grated
3 tablespoons mirin
1 teaspoon wasabi paste
1½ tablespoons soy sauce
⅓ cup water
¼ cup rice wine vinegar

1 Rinse rice in strainer under cold water until water runs clear. Place drained rice and the water in medium pot, cover tightly; bring to a boil. Reduce heat; simmer, covered tightly, about 12 minutes or until water is absorbed and rice is just cooked. Remove from heat; let rice stand, covered, for 10 minutes.

2 Meanwhile, whisk together ingredients for mirin and wasabi dressing.

3 Using vegetable peeler, slice cucumbers into ribbons. Slice daikon thinly; cut slices into matchstick-sized pieces. Combine rice, cucumber, and daikon in large bowl with lemon, fish, dressing, and half of the sesame seeds; toss gently to combine. Divide salad among serving bowls; top with seaweed and remaining sesame.

preparation time 25 minutes
cooking time 15 minutes
serves 4

per serving 13.3g fat; 735 cal

tip
Sticky rice, also known as koshihikari or Chinese sweet rice, is the very short-grained rice that is used in making sushi. If you can't find sticky rice you can use risotto rice.

garlic shrimp with citrus salad

20 uncooked jumbo shrimp
(3 pounds)
3 cloves garlic, crushed
2 teaspoons finely grated lime
peel
⅓ cup lime juice
3 tablespoons olive oil
2 small cucumbers, sliced thinly
8 ounces cherry tomatoes, halved
1 cup pitted kalamata olives
3 small oranges (about 1 pound),
segmented
1 medium red onion, halved,
sliced thickly
14 ounces baby curly endive,
trimmed, torn

LIME AND ORANGE DRESSING
2 teaspoons finely grated lime
peel
1½ tablespoons olive oil
¼ cup orange juice
¼ cup lime juice

1 Peel and devein shrimp, leaving tails intact. Combine in medium bowl with garlic, lime peel, lime juice, and oil; refrigerate 3 hours or overnight, turning occasionally.

2 Cook drained shrimp on heated oiled grill or grill pan until changed in color.

3 Whisk together lime and orange dressing.

4 Combine shrimp in large bowl with cucumbers, tomatoes, olives, oranges, onion, and dressing; toss gently to combine. Divide endive among serving plates; top with salad.

preparation time 30 minutes
(plus refrigeration time)
cooking time 10 minutes
serves 4

per serving 15.6g fat; 396 cal

glossary

barberries also known as zereshk, sold dried; dark red in color, slightly tart in flavor, and elongated in shape. Can be found in Middle Eastern food stores.

basil

purple also known as opal; has large purple leaves and a sweet, almost gingery flavor. Can be substituted for Thai basil.

Thai also known as horapa; has smallish leaves and sweet liquorice; one of the basic flavors of Thai cuisine.

beans

black also known as turtle beans; Cuban or Latin American rather than Chinese in origin.

black-eyed also known as black-eyed peas; are the dried seed of a variant of the snake or yard bean.

fava available dried, fresh, canned, or frozen. Fresh or frozen, they are best peeled twice, discarding both the outer long, green pod and the beige-green tough inner shell.

bell pepper come in many colors: red, green, yellow, purplish-black, and orange. Discard seeds and membrane before use.

bok choy has a fresh, mild mustard taste and is good braised or in stir-fries. Baby bok choy is smaller and more tender than bok choy.

breadcrumbs, stale one- or two-day-old bread made into crumbs by grating, blending, or processing.

bulgur wheat hulled, steamed wheat kernels that are dried and crushed into various-sized grains.

butternut squash can be used interchangeably with pumpkin. Butternut has a pear-shaped gourd with golden skin and orange flesh.

caperberries fruit formed after the caper buds have flowered; caperberries are pickled, usually with stalks intact.

capers the grey-green buds of a warm-climate (usually Mediterranean) shrub, sold either dried and salted or pickled in a vinegar brine. Baby capers, those picked early, are smaller, fuller-flavored, and more expensive than the full-sized ones. Capers should be rinsed well before using.

cayenne pepper a long, thin-fleshed, extremely hot red chili usually sold dried and ground.

celeriac tuberous root with brown skin, white flesh, and a celery-like flavor.

cheese

bocconcini walnut-sized, fresh baby mozzarella, a delicate, semi-soft, white cheese. Spoils rapidly so must be kept refrigerated, in its packing liquid, for one or two days at most.

feta a crumbly goat- or sheep-milk cheese with a sharp, salty taste.

goat made from goat milk, has an earthy, strong taste; available in soft and firm textures, in various shapes and sizes, sometimes rolled in herbs.

haloumi a firm, sheep-milk cheese matured in brine; somewhat like a minty, salty feta in flavor. Better suited for cooking than for eating on its own, haloumi can be grilled or fried, briefly, without it breaking down. It can be found in some delis, cheese shops, or Mediterranean markets.

mozzarella originally from southern Italy where it is traditionally made of water-buffalo milk. It's the traditional pizza cheese, becoming elastic when heated.

parmesan a hard, grainy cow-milk cheese that originated in the Parma region of Italy. The curd is salted in brine for a month before being aged for up to two years in humid conditions. Parmesan is mainly grated as a topping for pasta, soups, and other savory dishes, but is also delicious eaten with fruit.

ricotta the name for this moist, soft, white, sweet, cow-milk cheese translates as "cooked again." It's made from whey, a byproduct of cheese-making, to which fresh milk and acid are added. Has a low fat content and a slightly grainy texture.

chervil herb with mild fennel flavor and curly leaves.

chickpeas also called garbanzos; sandy-colored, round legume.

chili generally the smaller the chili, the hotter it is. Use rubber gloves when seeding and chopping fresh chilies to prevent skin burns.

flakes, dried deep-red, dehydrated chili slices and whole seeds; good for use in cooking or as a condiment for sprinkling over cooked foods.

red serrano or Thai small, very hot and bright red; substitute with habanero chilies.

Chinese barbecued pork traditionally cooked in special ovens, this has a sweet-sticky coating made from soy sauce, sherry, five-spice powder and hoisin sauce. Available from Asian food stores.

Chinese cabbage elongated in shape with pale green crinkly leaves, the most common cabbage in Southeast Asia. Can be eaten raw or braised, steamed, or stir-fried.

coconut milk not the juice found inside the fruit, but the diluted liquid pressed from the white meat of a mature coconut. After the liquid settles, the cream and "milk" (thin white fluid) separate naturally.

cilantro bright-green, leafy herb with a pungent flavor.

coriander the seeds, whole or ground, of the Cilantro plant.

cornstarch used as a thickening agent in all types of cooking.

couscous a fine, grain-like cereal product, originally from North Africa; made from semolina.

cumin resembling caraway in size, cumin is the dried seed of a plant related to parsley, having a spicy, nutty flavor. Available in seed form or dried and ground.

daikon also known as a giant white radish. Used extensively in Japanese cooking; has a sweet, fresh flavor without the bite of the common red radish. Can be used raw in salads and as a garnish, or cooked in various ways.

egg some recipes call for raw or barely cooked eggs; exercise caution if salmonella is a problem.

eggplant also known as aubergine; a purple-skinned vegetable that can also be bought char-grilled, packed in oil, and in glass jars.

endive, curly also known as frisée, a curly-leafed green vegetable, mainly used in salads.

fingerling potato small, finger-shaped potato with a nutty flavor.

fish sauce made from pulverized, salted, fermented fish. Has a pungent smell and strong taste; use sparingly.

five-spice powder fragrant ground mixture of cinnamon, clove, star anise, szechuan pepper, and fennel seeds.

green onion also known as scallion; an immature onion

picked before the bulb has formed; has a long, bright-green, edible stalk.

honeydew melon an oval fruit with a delicate taste and pale green flesh.

horseradish, prepared grated horseradish bottled in salt and vinegar.

kalamata olives small, sharp-tasting, brine-cured black olives.

kalonji also known as nigella; angular seeds, black on the outside and creamy within, with a sharp nutty flavor. Available in Middle Eastern markets.

kecap manis also known as ketjap manis; a thick soy sauce with added sugar and spices. You can buy it at Asian markets, or you can make your own by heating equal parts soy sauce, and brown sugar or molasses, stirring until molasses or sugar melts.

leek a member of the onion family; looks like a giant green onion but is more subtle and mild in flavor.

lemongrass a tall, sharp-edged grass tasting and smelling of lemon; only the white lower part of the stem is used. You can find it at Asian markets; buy it fresh.

linguine known as flat spaghetti or little tongues because of its shape.

mandoline originally from Italy, this kitchen tool is essential for the cook as it performs tasks nearly impossible to do with even the sharpest of knives: matchsticks, shoestrings, and paper-thin slices are achievable and all identical in size.

mango tropical fruit with fragrant, deep-yellow flesh surrounding a large, flat seed.

meat some recipes in this book call for raw or uncooked meat; exercise caution if there's a salmonella problem.

mesclun is a salad mix of young lettuce and other green leaves, including baby spinach, mizuna, curly endive, arugula, and young mustard greens.

mirin sweet Japanese rice wine used solely in cooking; not to be confused with sake, which is also used as a drink. Sweet sherry can be substituted but is fruitier.

mizuna Japanese in origin; frizzy salad leaf having a mustard flavor. Arugula or young mustard greens can be used instead.

mushrooms

button small, cultivated white mushrooms with a mild flavor; are available all year round.

cap slightly larger and has a stronger flavor than the button. Sometimes called cups, caps are firm textured and ideal for soups, pies, and casseroles.

portabella large, flat mushroom variety with a rich earthy flavor, ideal for filling and grilling.

oyster gray-white mushrooms shaped like a fan. Prized for

their smooth texture and subtle, oyster-like flavor.

porcini earthy-flavored and aromatic, available both fresh and dried; the latter are reconstituted and used in many classic Italian dishes such as risottos and pasta sauces.

mustard

Dijon a pale brown, distinctively flavored, fairly mild french mustard.

English, mild less pungent version of the traditional hot variety of English mustard.

whole-grain a coarse-grained mustard made from black and yellow mustard seeds and a dijon-style mustard.

noodles

egg made from wheat flour and eggs, sold fresh or dried. They range in size from very fine strands to wide spaghetti-like pieces as thick as a shoelace.

rice soft, white noodles made from rice flour and vegetable oil; available in varying thicknesses, from vermicelli-thin to broad and flat. Rinse under hot water to remove starch and excess oil before using.

paprika ground dried bell pepper, available in four varieties: mild, hot, sweet, and smoked.

pastrami a highly seasoned, cured, and smoked beef, usually cut from the round; ready to eat when purchased.

pawpaw also known as papaya or papaw; large, pear-shaped, red-orange tropical fruit. Sometimes used unripe (green) in salads and stir-fries.

pepitas dried squash seeds

pine nuts not, in fact, a nut but the small, cream-colored kernel of a pine cone.

pita this wheat-flour pocket bread is sold in large, flat pieces that separate into two thin rounds. Also available in small thick pieces called pocket pita.

polenta a flour-like cereal made of dried corn sold ground in different textures; also the name of the dish made from it.

preserved lemon a North African specialty, the citrus is preserved, usually whole, in a mixture of salt and lemon juice. Can be rinsed and eaten as is, or added to casseroles and stews to impart a rich, salty-sour, acidic flavor. Can be difficult to find in the United States.

rice vermicelli a kind of noodle used throughout Southeast Asia in spring rolls and cold salads; similar to bean threads, only longer and made with rice flour instead of mung bean starch.

rice, sticky (koshihikari) small, round-grain white rice. Substitute short-grain white rice and cook by the absorption method.

risoni small, rice-shaped pasta very similar to another small pasta, orzo, which can be used as a substitute.

sake rice wine used in cooking or as a drink. If unavailable, substitute dry sherry or brandy.

sambal oelek Indonesian, this salty paste is made from ground chili. You can find it in Asian markets.

sashimi a Japanese style of eating raw fish; use caution if a salmonella problem exists.

scallop a bivalve mollusk with a fluted shell valve.

seafood some recipes in this book call for raw or uncooked fish and other seafood; exercise caution if there is a salmonella problem.

sesame seeds black and white are the most common of this small oval seed; however, there are also red and brown varieties.

shallots small, brown-skinned, elongated members of the onion family. Grow in tight clusters similarly to garlic.

snow peas also called mange tout ("eat all" in French). Its almost translucent, bright green pod is thin and crisp.

soy sauce, Japanese less dense and salty than Chinese soy.

spinach tender, green leaves are good uncooked in salads or eaten on their own as a cooked vegetable. Baby spinach leaves are even more tender and can be added to a dish just before serving.

sumac a purple-red, astringent spice ground from the berry of a shrub that grows wild around the eastern Mediterranean; adds a tart, lemony flavor to dips and dressings, and goes well with barbecued meat. Available from Middle Eastern food stores.

star anise dried star-shaped fruit of a tree native to China. The pods, which have an astringent aniseed-like flavor, are widely used in Asian cooking. Available whole or ground.

tahini sesame seed paste available from Middle Eastern food stores; often used in hummus and baba ghanoush.

tat soi (Chinese flat cabbage) can be found at most local greengrocers as well as Asian supermarkets.

toasted seaweed dried seaweed used in Japanese cooking as a flavoring, garnish, or for sushi. Sold in thin sheets.

tofu, firm compressed bean curd with most of the water extracted. Good in stir-fries because it does not fall apart when tossed.

tomato

cherry small and round.

roma a type of plum tomato, these are oval-shaped.

paste triple-concentrated tomato purée used to flavor soups and sauces.

tortillas thin, round unleavened bread originating in Mexico; can be purchased frozen, fresh, or vacuum-packed. They are made of either wheat or cornstarch.

vinegar

apple cider made from fermented apples.

balsamic originally from Modena, Italy, there are many balsamic vinegars, ranging in pungency and quality depending on how long they have been aged. Quality can be determined up to a point by price; use expensive balsamic sparingly.

raspberry made from fresh raspberries steeped in a white wine vinegar.

red wine based on fermented red wine.

rice a colorless vinegar made from fermented rice and flavored with sugar and salt. Also known as seasoned rice vinegar.

sherry natural vinegar aged in oak according to the traditional spanish winemaking process.

white wine based on fermented white wine; a very mellow wine vinegar.

v-slicer a classic German kitchen tool used for slicing, shredding, dicing, julienning, and cutting fresh vegetables and fruits. Prized for its speed and precision.

wasabi an Asian horseradish used to make the pungent green sauce traditionally served with Japanese raw fish dishes; sold in powdered or paste form.

index

conversion chart

measures

The difference between one country's measuring cups and another's is, at most, within a 2 or 3 teaspoon variance, and will not affect your cooking results. All cup and spoon measurements are level. The most accurate way of measuring dry ingredients is to weigh them. When measuring liquids, use a clear glass or plastic jug with graduated markings.

We use large eggs with an average weight of 2oz.

dry measures

IMPERIAL	METRIC
½oz	15g
1oz	30g
2oz	60g
3oz	90g
4oz (¼lb)	125g
5oz	155g
6oz	185g
7oz	220g
8oz (½lb)	250g
9oz	280g
10oz	315g
11oz	345g
12oz (¾lb)	375g
13oz	410g
14oz	440g
15oz	470g
16oz (1lb)	500g
24oz (1½lb)	750g
32oz (2lb)	1kg

liquid measures

IMPERIAL	METRIC
1 fluid oz	30ml
2 fluid oz	60ml
3 fluid oz	100ml
4 fluid oz	125ml
5 fluid oz (¼ pint/1 gill)	150ml
6 fluid oz	190ml
8 fluid oz	250ml
16 fluid oz (1 pint)	500ml
1 quart	1000ml (1 litre)

length measures

IMPERIAL	METRIC
⅛in	3mm
¼in	6mm
½in	1cm
¾in	2cm
1in	2.5cm
2in	5cm
2½in	6cm
3in	8cm
4in	10cm
5in	13cm
6in	15cm
7in	18cm
8in	20cm
9in	23cm
10in	25cm
11in	28cm
12in (1ft)	30cm

oven temperatures

These oven temperatures are only a guide for conventional ovens. For fan-forced ovens, check the manufacturer's manual.

	°C (CELSIUS)	°F (FAHRENHEIT)
Very slow	120	250
Slow	150	275-300
Moderately slow	160	325
Moderate	180	350-375
Moderately hot	200	400
Hot	220	425-450
Very hot	240	475